All rights reserved.

Copyright © 2024 Uma K. Tapia

Effortless Mediterranean Recipes Ready for You : Delicious Mediterranean Dishes Made Simple for Your Kitchen

Funny helpful tips:

Nurture love daily; it's the foundation of a lasting relationship.

Rotate between different authors within a genre; it provides varied styles and perspectives.

Introduction

This book provides an in-depth exploration of the Mediterranean diet, a renowned eating plan celebrated for its health benefits. It begins by introducing readers to the essence of the Mediterranean diet, emphasizing the importance of specific nutrients like fiber, vitamins, minerals, antioxidants, and less sugar in the diet. The guide highlights the numerous health benefits associated with this dietary approach, including heart health, brain health, blood sugar control, cancer prevention, weight management, and more.

Key ingredients that form the foundation of the Mediterranean diet are elaborated upon, helping readers understand what makes this diet unique. Pantry staples essential for Mediterranean cuisine are detailed, offering valuable insights into the ingredients required to prepare delicious and nutritious meals.

To make the Mediterranean diet more accessible, the guide provides a shopping list, making it easier for readers to stock up on the necessary items. Sticking to this diet is made simpler with a set of rules and tips, such as following the Harvard Ratio, incorporating sheep and goat cheese, increasing fish consumption, replacing refined grains with whole grains, limiting red meat intake, and focusing on seasonal vegetables.

The cookbook covers various meal categories, including breakfast, lunch, dinner, and desserts. It offers a wide array of recipes inspired by the Mediterranean diet, allowing readers to enjoy the flavors and health benefits associated with this culinary tradition. Whether you're looking for breakfast ideas to start your day right or seeking savory dinner options that align with the Mediterranean diet, this cookbook provides a diverse range of recipes to suit various tastes and preferences.

Overall, this book serves as an informative and practical guide for individuals interested in adopting the Mediterranean diet and enjoying its numerous health advantages. With its emphasis on key nutrients, ingredients, and a variety of delicious recipes, this cookbook is a valuable resource for anyone looking to make positive dietary changes in pursuit of a healthier lifestyle.

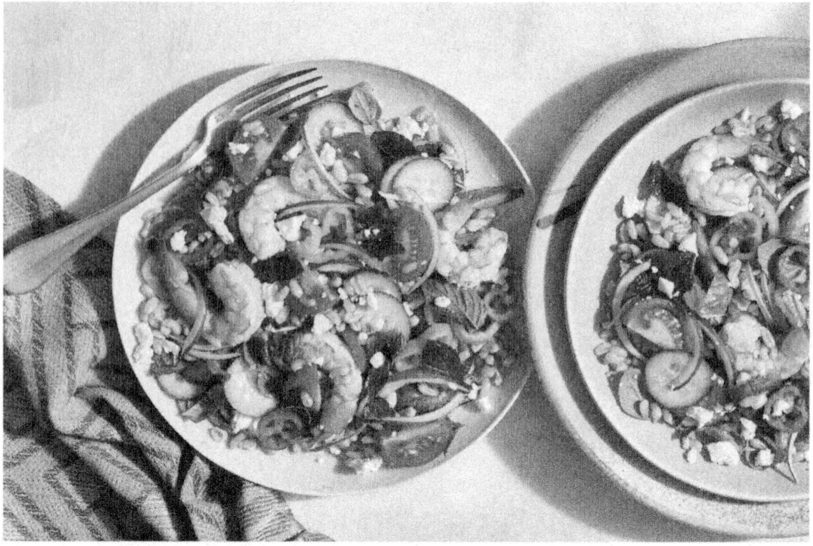

Contents

What is the Mediterranean diet? 1
Nutrients in the Mediterranean diet 4
    Fiber 4
    Vitamins and minerals 4
    Antioxidants 5
    Less sugar 5
Health Benefits of the Mediterranean diet 6
    It keeps the heart-healthy. 6
    It keeps your brain healthy. 6
    It keeps your mind healthy. 6
    It keeps your blood sugar in control. 6
    It keeps away cancer. 7
    It keeps your weight in check. 7
    It's great for old age women. 7
    It keeps the digestive tract healthy 7
    It helps you to live longer. 8
Key Ingredients of the Mediterranean Diet 9
    Olives 0
    Wheat 9
    Green vegetables 10
    Chickpeas 10
    Garlic 10
    Herbs and Spices 10
    Cheese and Yogurt 11

- Must have Pantry staples for the Mediterranean diet 11
  - Extra Virgin Olive Oil 11
  - Canned fish 11
  - Dried fruits 12
  - Nuts 12
  - Whole grains Staples 12
  - Tomatoes 12
  - Olives 12
  - Whole-grain crackers 13
  - Canned beans 13
  - Herbs and Spices 13
  - Greek yogurt 13
  - Cheese 14
- Shopping List for the Mediterranean Diet 15
  - Fruits: 16
  - Dairy Products: 16
  - Meat and Poultry: 17
  - Fish and Seafood: 17
  - Grains and Bread: 17
  - Fats and Nuts: 17
  - Beans: 18
  - Pantry Items: 18
  - Herbs and Spices: 18
- Rules for Sticking To the MediterraneanDiet 20
  - Follow Harvard Ratio 20
  - Use sheep and goats cheese. 20
  - Consume Fresh Fish more than once in a week. 21

Completely replace your refined grain stocks with whole grains. 21

Red meat should be rarely eaten. 21

Eat seasonal vegetables. 22

Shakshuka 25

Avocado Toast with Cream Cheese 27

Mediterranean Egg Casserole 29

Spinach, Tomato, and Feta Scrambled Eggs 32

Quinoa with Berries 34

Muesli 36

Mediterranean Breakfast Quinoa 38

Spinach and Feta Egg Wrap 40

Greek Salad 46

White Bean Salad 48

Mediterranean Couscous Salad 50

Baked Parmesan Zucchini 52

Fish Sticks 54

Falafel 56

Roasted Tomato and Basil Soup 59

Mediterranean Tuna Salad 62

Italian Baked Chicken 64

Stuffed Champignon Mushrooms 66

Prosciutto and Arugula Pizza 68

Chicken and Spinach Pasta 70

Mediterranean Quinoa Salad 72

Penne with Shrimp 74

Salmon Soup 78

Greek Black Eyed Peas 80

Baked Cod with Garlic and Lemon 82

Greek Chicken Souvlaki 84

Grilled Swordfish 86

Mediterranean Stuffed Chicken Breasts 88

Greek Cauliflower Rice Bowls with Chicken 90

Chicken Parmesan Pasta 92

Mediterranean Chicken and Chickpea Soup 94

Chicken Piccata 96

Greek Turkey Burgers 98

Greek Chicken Soup with Lemon 101

Shrimp Spaghetti 103

Yogurt and Honey Olive Oil Cake 109

Apple and Nuts with Whipped Yogurt 111

Whole Grain Muffins with Citrus and Olive Oil 113

Baked Pears with Maple and Vanilla 115

Chocolate Mousse with Greek Yogurt 117

Strawberry Popsicles 119

Mint Chocolate Chip Ice Cream 121

Chocolate and Avocado Pudding 123

Matcha and Blueberry Crisp 125

Conclusion 127

What is the Mediterranean diet?

Many Magazines and Health Professionals claim the Mediterranean diet as the best diet plan available. The popularity around the topic started in the late 20th century. After a great deal of literature and reproducible studies, it has taken the number one spot among all the diet plans. If you want a fulfilling, disease avoiding, easy following, and nutritious diet plan, then you have to look no further.

It is inspired by the lifestyle and eating patterns of the people living in countries surrounding the Mediterranean Sea. The most noteworthy countries are Greece, Italy, Turkey, and France. The diet came into people's attention when papers and studies were published during the 1950s and 60s, showing a reduction in cardiovascular diseases in seven different countries in the region. These studies started because a doctor in Naples, a city in Italy, reported no cardiovascular-related cases at his hospital.

Mediterranean diet doesn't have a strict set of rules but guidelines that make you eat healthily. How does it do this? It makes you eat more vegetables and fruits of a diverse variety. It replaces your main protein intakes from red meat and eggs to fish, beans, and pulses, although you can consume eggs in moderation. Animal or saturated fats are primarily replaced by healthy unsaturated fats and Omega fatty acids. This is done by eating a lot of fish and olive oil compared to other sources of fat. Processed or "white" flour and rice are replaced by whole grains, which is ideal because refined grains make you more at risk with diseases. It doesn't prohibit eating dairy, snacks, and drinking wine but advises to do it in moderation. This is the general foundation that makes up this diet. Your main choice for liquids will become water when following this diet, and sugary drinks are not prohibited, but they are extremely discouraged.

There might be a better diet for weight loss or a particular organ, but the Mediterranean diet is a choice for overall healthy eating. There are a lot of ways it refines the body. It helps maintain mental health as it shows improvement in Alzheimer's and Parkinson's studies, it reduces the chances of type-2 diabetes and hypertension, two of the most prominent co-morbidities. It reduces the chances of obesity by decreasing excess carbohydrate and fat intake. These are just a few of the advantages they can give.

The most important reason why it is said to be the best diet of today is the ease in following and maintaining it. Studies have shown that fast diet plans that make a person starve and reduce weight quickly do not help the individual in the long run because they almost always revert to their routine and gain even more pounds, which are harder to shed. You can say that you will never eat carbohydrates again, but that is impossible if you are not extremely strong-willed. The diet gives maximum benefits with very low stress on the individual following it. Trendy diet plans always lose in experts' opinions because they are not researched well enough, and most of them don't let you indulge. A healthy diet should never restrict someone completely from any food.

Ten commandments of the Mediterranean diet

There are only ten guidelines that you have to follow to start your dieting journey.

1. Avoid using processed foods and always cook your meal.
2. Eat fresh, local, and seasonal vegetables and fruits. Opt for a diverse variety instead of sticking to a few selections.
3. Eat a lot more fish and beans to have a steady supply of protein. Seldom use eggs and chicken.

4. Eat a lot more whole grains and potatoes to give you your daily energy requirements.
5. Use dairy products in moderation but eat one form of it daily. Cheese is preferable than its other forms, especially goat and sheep cheese.
6. Eat a lot less red meats, and if you plan to, mix other ingredients as well.
7. Make all of your meals vegetable centered.
8. Use olive oil abundantly.
9. Have fruits in the form of desserts every day. Have a snack occasionally, but fruits should dominate.
10. Drink a lot of water to stay hydrated all day.

Nutrients in the Mediterranean diet

The Mediterranean diet focuses on vegetables, so it contains a significant level of nutrition; many other advantages are seen by encouraging us to do smart cooking and eating choices. The diet contains an array of food groups filling us with sustenance.

Here are some of the most important nutrients that this diet provides.

Good Fats

The average person eats a lot of cholesterol and saturated fatty acids. Eating fried, fast foods, and using animal fats only damages our body. It is linked to heart disease and higher levels of cardiovascular problems. This diet switches the saturated fatty acids with monounsaturated fatty acids that lower the chances of these diseases.

Fiber

The diet encourages the use of vegetables, fruits, and whole grains. All of them lead to high consumption of dietary fiber. It makes it less likely for bowel cancer and other intestinal diseases to occur. Also, it helps digestion and may also reduce the chances of type 2 diabetes. It promotes satiety, which prevents overeating

Vitamins and minerals

Almost all the daily requirements of different vitamins and minerals are fulfilled in this diet. Vegetables and fruits are naturally rich in these substances. A vitamin that is not found in them is Vitamin B12, which can only come from animal sources. A strict vegetarian diet might pose these problems, but not this one. In the Mediterranean diet, you are encouraged to eat lots of fish, and an abundant supply of it can be found in salmon, trout, and tuna.

Antioxidants

Vegetables and fruits are the main sources of antioxidants. They are substances that remove free radicals from our body, reducing the chances of cancer and many other problems. They are consumed in high quantities if you are following the diet's guidelines.

Less sugar

There is added sugar in every product that we buy. Sugars are the main culprit of obesity and its associated diseases. Lowering the consumption of sweets and snacks and replacing them with fruits can help elevate your health. Fruits have sugars in them, but they are also highly nutritious, so eating them in moderation is a smart choice.

Health Benefits of the Mediterranean diet

It keeps the heart-healthy.

The reason why it came to the public eye in the first place was its ability to reduce problems associated with the heart. It reduces the risk of heart diseases and stroke, decreasing the chance of early death. The diet promotes the use of fish and vegetables, a source of Omega fats and antioxidants, the nutrients keeping your heart beating smoothly.

It keeps your brain healthy.

Numerous studies show that if you follow the Mediterranean diet and have a high fish intake, you are less likely to get Alzheimer's and other old age mental diseases. A study consisting of almost 2000 participants found that people following the diet were less likely to develop cognitive disorders.

It keeps your mind healthy.

Psychiatrists all around the globe give their patients the advice to change their diet. A bad high fatty or sugary diet is linked with a negative mental state. Carotenoids in different vegetables and fruits change the bacterial population in our gut, boosting our mood. A study found that following a Mediterranean diet reduces the chances of depression.

It keeps your blood sugar in control.

Unlike many other diets, the Mediterranean diet doesn't just lower your carbohydrate intake, leaving you sluggish and tired. It encourages the person to eat alt of whole grains such as quinoa, buckwheat, etc. They maintain blood sugar levels and do not make you feel that you are compromising your energy.

It keeps away cancer.

Studies with over 2 million subjects have shown that the Mediterranean diet is the best diet to prevent cancer from developing. A good dose of antioxidants is taken every day, helping the body remove harmful chemicals.

It keeps your weight in check.

The Mediterranean diet contains rich and diverse food choices and prohibits no food group, which makes weight loss easy. The person eats more fiber and whole grains, which promotes satiety and maintains our energy. We do not feel hungry as often as we might be if we eat junk food regularly.

It's great for old age women.

Postmenopausal women experience a decline in their bone strength and muscle mass, which leads to injuries and low quality of life. A study suggests that the diet may prevent this issue in the long term and reduce bones and muscles' loss.

It keeps the digestive tract healthy.

A study found that people who follow a diet containing high fruits and vegetables increase the bacteria's quality in their gut significantly. The number of good bacteria is very high when you follow the Mediterranean diet as well. The Diet of traditional Westerners is not healthy and very bad for the intestines.

It helps you to live longer.

All the benefits combined, it produces a collective result of increasing longevity and decreasing mortality rate. It is mainly due to the prevention of diabetes and heart problems. Mediterranean countries contain longer living people, and the diet is the reason for their excellent health.

Key Ingredients of the Mediterranean Diet

Mediterranean diet depends upon home cooking and consuming seasonal vegetables and fruits. Some ingredients can change based on the area's food supplies, but some key ingredients stay the same no matter where you are. Here is a list of some of them below:

Olive oil

One of the main guidelines in the diet is to use olive oil generously. Italy and Greece, two major Mediterranean countries, produce the largest amount of olive oil and consume a lot of it as well. It is highly nutritious, with carotenoids, tocopherols, and antioxidants present in it. It advances the flavor of vegetables, which makes the person prefer them more. You can use it for cooking, baking, and as a dressing.

Olives

Dipping sauce and paste often contain a large number of olives in the Mediterranean region. They are pitted and put into various dishes as toppings or main ingredients. They obtain high levels of polyphenols and antioxidants, which makes them very healthy.

Wheat

It dominates the Mediterranean plate, and you cannot successfully follow the diet without it. The Mediterranean diet uses unrefined wheat and barley flour for their bread and main source of carbohydrate. Durum is also very popular in the Mediterranean region and is used for making bread and couscous. It is high in fiber and has a low glycemic index, which prevents obesity and overeating while controlling your sugar levels.

Green vegetables

The Mediterranean region has a high consumption of different types of vegetables, especially green vegetables. Dandelion greens, arugula, and fennel are just some examples of more than a hundred greens available. They all are rich in flavonoids, but different vegetables each bring something special to the nutrient table. It's important to eat a diverse variety. It is also a rich source of calcium, magnesium, and iron.

Chickpeas

In the Mediterranean diet, chickpeas play an important part. Just one cup or 82 grams of chickpeas provides a high amount of fibers, magnesium, folate, protein, and dietary fiber. It is used in many dishes as a garnish or as a main ingredient. Chickpeas, fava beans, and lentils should all be consumed either cooked or baked form.

Garlic

Garlic is used as a seasoning in many Mediterranean dishes. You can use it inside a sauce and have your many dishes beside it. It is a well-known anti-inflammatory ingredient, and it also prevents cancer and the flu. Aioli is also a popular source that contains garlic.

Herbs and Spices

Every Mediterranean country has its palate and, by contrast, has its variety of herbs and spices. Almost in all of them, they play an important role in seasoning meals. They are high in antioxidants, anti-inflammatory compounds, and phenols. Fresh herbs are a significant source of flavor and nutrition.

Cheese and Yogurt

Many sauces, salads, and meals contain yogurt and cheese to raise the dish's flavor in these regions. They are filled with probiotics and are a source of proteins. Yogurt and cheese are traditional ingredients of this region, and the diet will not be complete without them.

Must have Pantry staples for the Mediterranean diet

The Mediterranean diet makes you eat lots of vegetables, fish, and fruits, but some items can even further elevate the meals. Here is a list of items you can keep in your kitchen cabinets to have an excellent dieting experience.

Extra Virgin Olive Oil

In the Mediterranean diet, olive oil is used for cooking and frying. It can also be consumed as a dressing. It is incredibly healthy, a good source of good fats, and provides tons of flavors. It also has a high smoking point for a better cooking experience.

Canned fish

Fresh fishes are a must if you follow the diet, but having canned fishes stored can be a great benefit. It can be used to make many small and sided dishes. Canned sardines, anchovies, and clams can be used alongside or separate from fresh fish. It adds variety and increases omega-3 intake.

Dried fruits

Buy some different dried fruits from the store or make some added home; these ingredients will significantly elevate your dishes' flavors. Apricots and berries can bring sweet and savory notes; raisins and prunes can be used as well. Fruits are extremely healthy. Serve them beside your dish and eat with joy.

Nuts

They are healthy; provide a great variety of flavors and texture. They can be sprinkled over salads, be made into relish, and be used in combination with other nuts to make a dish independently. There are many choices among nuts; walnuts, peanuts, almonds, tahini, pine nuts, etc. All of them can be used to raise the quality of the dish.

Whole grains Staples

They are the backbone of this diet, providing the main source of energy and filling our appetite. Get some buckwheat, corn grits, faro millet, etc. Get any whole grains that you like and stock on it to have a plentiful supply of it for a long time.

Tomatoes

Be it dried or canned, tomatoes can be used in various ways to make a dish. It can become the main ingredient or provide flavor. It is available almost everywhere and is used all year round. You can add it in pasta and stews to make a thicker and more satiating base.

Olives

Olives are a favorite of the Mediterranean region. There are many types of them, bringing different flavors, and they are very healthy. One of the most liked is Castelvetranos, which gives a buttery taste. They can be sprinkled, used in the dressing, or blended in a sauce for use.

Whole-grain crackers

You will need some snacks to curb your cravings or prevent you from digging into the store-bought chips and sweets. Whole-grain crackers give a much better taste than white grained ones and go excellent with cheeses. They are also quite healthy when compared to other snacks.

Canned beans

Fresh beans should be the first choice, but you need to be prepared even for hectic rushed meals when you start a diet. They can expand the flavor and texture profile of your diet. You can get kidney beans, fava beans, lentils, etc.

Herbs and Spices

They are important for any meal and are used worldwide to bring up the taste of other ingredients. The spices and herbs you can use are oregano, dill, sage, thyme, black pepper, cumin, basil leaves, garlic powder, ginger powder, paprika, etc.

Greek yogurt

It is a great source of protein and can be used to make an array of dishes and meals. Its versatility can be used to elevate any type of recipe in any way we desire to. It can be used in savory or sweet dishes.

Cheese

In this diet, you are required to eat plentiful cheese, so it's obvious that you should stock up on it. It can be served deliciously alongside whole grains, bread, and roasted potatoes. There are plentiful choices in this category as well, so mix and experiment with different flavors.

Shopping List for the Mediterranean Diet

Shopping list items vary from country to country, and also items change according to seasons. Your first choice should be seasonal and local ingredients. No need to buy fancy and expensive imported ingredients. Here is a basic list mentioned below:

Vegetables:

- Tomatoes
- Peppers
- Onion
- Eggplant
- Cucumber
- Green beans
- Okra
- Zucchini
- Garlic
- Peas
- Potatoes
- Mushrooms
- Cauliflower
- Broccoli
- Carrots
- Celery
- Beets
- Spinach
- Cabbage

Frozen vegetables can also be used
Greens form an important component of the diet.

- Chicory
- Dandelions
- Beet greens
- Amaranth

Fruits:

Citrus fruits should dominate your plate but also keep eating a mixed variety.

- Orange
- Lemons
- Apples
- Pears
- Cherries
- Watermelon
- Cantaloupe
- Peaches
- Pears
- Figs
- Apricots

Dairy Products:

Full-fat dairy should be the first choice.

- Plain Greek yogurt
- Sheep's milk yogurt
- Feta cheese
- Fresh cheese like ricotta
- Parmesan
- Mozzarella
- Graviera
- Mizithra

Meat and Poultry:

They should be eaten rarely, like once a week.

- Chicken
- Beef
- Veal
- Pork

Fish and Seafood:

Preferably eat small fatty fish. You can eat canned fish as well.

- Anchovies
- Sardines
- Shrimp
- Calamari

Grains and Bread:

- Whole grain bread
- Whole grain breadsticks
- Pita bread
- Phyllo
- Pasta
- Rice
- Bulgur
- Couscous

Fats and Nuts:

- Extra virgin olive oil
- Tahini

- Almonds
- Walnuts
- Pine nuts
- Pistachios
- Sesame seeds

Beans:

- Lentils
- Chickpeas
- White Beans
- Fava Beans

Pantry Items:

- Canned tomatoes
- Olives
- Sun-dried tomatoes
- Capers
- Honey

Herbs and Spices:

- Oregano
- Parsley
- Dill
- Mint
- Basil
- Cumin
- Allspice
- Cinnamon
- Pepper

- Sea salt
- Sage
- Thyme
- Herbal Tea

Rules for Sticking To the Mediterranean Diet

There are no restrictions, you can go as slow or strict as you like, but this flexibility might be confusing you on how to start the diet. Here are some suggestions that you might find helpful.

Switch to olive oil instead of butter

Olive oil is extremely healthy, filled with phenols and good fats. The monounsaturated fatty acids are shown to reduce weight and keep the waistline in check. In the past decades, fat has been under fire, but it is still an essential part of a balanced diet. Olive oil and avocado oil are high in calories, but they provide energy and lower bad cholesterol.

Follow Harvard Ratio

The diet is widespread and is being studied worldwide. Scientists at Harvard have also taken their interest in the diet and came up with an ingredient to plate ratio that gives maximum benefit to the dieter. The ratio is :

- Fill half of your plate with vegetables (½)
- Fill one-fourth of your plate with grains (¼)
- Fill one-fourth of your plate with protein(¼)

If you want to lose weight, you have to control your proportion sizes effectively. An incredibly easy way to do this is by using smaller plates. You don't want to count calories in this diet.

Use sheep and goats cheese.

People living in the Mediterranean region love their cheeses. Even if they use it a lot, sheep's and goat's cheese are considered healthier because they have medium and not long fatty acid chains. Some examples of this kind of cheeses are Halloumi, Feta, Ricotta, Manchego, Roquefort, Pecorino, etc. They are a good source of calcium and healthy for bones.

Consume Fresh Fish more than once in a week.

You need to cook small oily fishes. They have been shown to reduce deadly diseases. Some examples of these kinds of fish include mackerel, sardines, tuna, herring, and trout. There are lots of ways to prepare them, baking, curing, frying, and grilling. You can make them into a stew or even roost it.

Completely replace your refined grain stocks with whole grains.

Refined grains have been linked to many diseases. These grains lose their fiber content when processed, making them less nutritious and less fulfilling. The person gets hungry quickly and overeats. Eat whole grains as much as possible as they are the main supply of your energy and carbohydrates.

Red meat should be rarely eaten.

Red meat and mortality studies show that eating regular red meat leads to a higher chance of early death. If you are an extreme meat-eater, it's better to start slow and cut out one red meat meal every week until no meals surround it. If you are going to consume it, make it a side ingredient.

Eat seasonal vegetables.

Going to the market with an open mind will help you in your journey of successful dieting. Eating seasonal will make you eat a "rainbow," meaning vegetables of all colors. Each vegetable comes with its benefits, and it's important we consume all of them. Eating seasonal is the way to follow a good Mediterranean diet.

Breakfast

Egg Muffins

Prep Time:	10 minutes	Calories:	67
Cook Time:	35 minutes	Fat (g):	5
Total Time:	45 minutes	Protein (g):	4.7
Servings:	12	Carbs:	1.3

These muffins are extremely healthy, filled with eggs, veggies, and herbs. It's a great way to use leftover chicken and also impress your family.

Ingredients:

- Chicken, boneless, cooked, shredded — 4 oz (113 g)
- Chopped red bell pepper — ¾ cup
- 12

- Cherry tomatoes, halved   2
- Scallions, peeled, chopped   6
- Kalamata olives, pitted, chopped   1/3 teaspoon
- Salt   ¼ teaspoon
- Ground black pepper   ½ teaspoon
- Paprika   ¼ teaspoon
- Ground turmeric   ½ cup
- Parsley leaves, fresh, chopped   ¼ cup
- Feta cheese, crumbled   8
- Eggs

Instructions:

1. Switch on the oven, then set it to 350 degrees F (177°C) and let it preheat.
2. Meanwhile, take a 12-cup muffin pan, grease its cups with oil, and then divide scallions, tomatoes, olives, peppers, chicken, parsley, and cheese evenly among the cups.
3. Take a large bowl, crack the eggs in it, add salt, black pepper, and all the spices and then whisk until combined.
4. Pour the egg mixture over vegetables in each muffin cup and then bake for 35 minutes until muffins have set.
5. When done, take out muffins from the cups and then serve.

Shakshuka

Prep Time:	5 minutes	Calories:	304
Cook Time:	25 minutes	Fat (g):	18.1
Total Time:	30 minutes	Protein (g):	14.3
Servings:	4	Carbs:	23.1

Made with eggs resting on top of tomatoes and veggies, this dish is packed with flavors. It's an easy one-skillet dish.

Ingredients:

- Large white onion, peeled, chopped — 1
- Red bell peppers, chopped — 2
- Minced garlic — 1 tablespoon
- Ground coriander — 1 teaspoon

- Sweet paprika — 1 teaspoon
- Cumin, ground — ½ teaspoon
- Red pepper flakes — 1/8 teaspoon
- Salt — ½ teaspoon
- Ground black pepper — 1/3 teaspoon
- Chopped tomatoes — 6 cups
- Tomato sauce — ½ cup
- Eggs — 5
- Chopped parsley leaves, fresh — ¼ cup
- Chopped mint leaves, fresh — ¼ cup
- Olive oil — 3 tablespoons

Instructions:

1. Take a large skillet pan, place it over medium heat, add oil and when hot, add onion, garlic, and bell pepper and then stir in salt, black pepper, and all the spices.
2. Cook the vegetables for 5 minutes until soften, then add tomatoes and tomato sauce, stir until mixed and simmer for 10 minutes, covering the pan with its lid.
3. After 10 minutes, uncover the pan, continue cooking the tomato mixture until slightly thickened, then make five wells into it and crack an egg in each well.
4. Switch heat to the low level, cover the skillet with its lid and then cook for 5 to 8 minutes until egg whites have set.
5. Remove pan from heat, sprinkle mint and parsley on top, and then serve with bread.

Avocado Toast with Cream Cheese

Prep Time:	5 minutes	Calories:	188
Cook Time:	2 minutes	Fat (g):	8.7
Total Time:	7 minutes	Protein (g):	8
Servings:	1	Carbs:	22.3

Eat this toast for breakfast, lunch, or snack. Creamy avocados and yummy cheese will make you salivate for a long time.

Ingredients:

- Slice of whole-wheat toast — 1
- Flaxseed oil — 2 teaspoons
- Avocado, peeled, sliced, or mashed — ½
- Cream cheese — 1/3 cup

- Small tomato, sliced   1

- Basil leaves   As needed for serving

- Sesame seeds   1 teaspoon

Instructions:

1. Drizzle oil on both sides of bread and then toast for 1 to 2 minutes per side until golden brown.
2. Assemble the toast and for this, place the bread on a plate, sprinkle cheese on top, and then cover with the layer with avocado and tomato.
3. Scatter basil leaves on top, drizzle with some more oil and sesame seeds, and then serve.

Mediterranean Egg Casserole

Prep Time:	15 minutes	Calories:	310
Cook Time:	10 h and 10 min	Fat (g):	19
Total Time:	10 h and 25 min	Protein (g):	18
Servings:	10	Carbs:	14

This is a hearty and filling slow-cooked Mediterranean casserole is made for curbing your cravings. Eggs and veggies make it healthy and delicious.

Ingredients:

- Prosciutto, cut into 1/2-inch thick slices (you can use chicken instead) — 2 oz (57 g)
- Butter, unsalted — 1 tablespoon
- Cremini mushrooms, sliced — 3 cups

- Chopped red bell pepper — ½ cup
- Diced hash brown potatoes — 16 oz (454 g)
- Chopped spinach, fresh or frozen, thawed, moisture squeezed — 10 oz (283 g)
- Artichoke hearts, fresh or frozen, thawed, quartered — 1 cup
- Sun-dried tomato, chopped — 1/4 cup
- Cream Cheese — 8 oz (227 g)
- Cheddar cheese, shredded — 4 oz (113 g)
- Salt — to taste
- Black pepper — to taste
- Eggs — 8
- Dijon mustard — 1 tablespoon
- Whole milk — 2 cups

Instructions:

1. Take a large skillet pan, place it over medium-high heat and when hot, add prosciutto slices and then cook for 3 to 4 minutes until crisp. Transfer prosciutto to a plate.
2. Add butter to the pan and when it melts, add mushrooms and peppers and then cook for 4 minutes or until softened.
3. Plug in a 4-quarts slow cooker, grease it with oil, add potatoes and then layer with half of the tomatoes-artichokes mixture and half of the spinach.
4. Sprinkle with half of the cream cheese, layer with remaining vegetables, spinach, and cream cheese.
5. Crack eggs in a bowl, add mustard, prosciutto pieces, pour in the milk, season with salt and black pepper, whisk until blended, and then pour over

vegetables and cream cheese in the slow cooker. Then sprinkle the top with Cheddar cheese.
6. Shut the slow cooker with its lid and then cook for 4 to 5 hours at high heat setting or for 8 to 10 hours at low heat setting until eggs have set.
7. When done, let the casserole rest in the slow cooker for 10 minutes, then take it out and cut it into ten slices.
8. Enjoy!

Spinach, Tomato, and Feta Scrambled Eggs

Prep Time:	5 minutes	Calories:	199
Cook Time:	4 minutes	Fat (g):	16
Total Time:	9 minutes	Protein (g):	11.4
Servings:	2	Carbs:	2.4

A classic breakfast of scrambled eggs made with plentiful veggies. The Mediterranean taste also comes from delicious feta cheese.

Ingredients:

- Olive oil — 1 tablespoon
- Tomato, seeded, diced — 1/3 cup
- Baby spinach — 1 cup
- Eggs — 3

- Feta cheese, cubed   2 tablespoons
- Salt   ¼ teaspoon
- Ground black pepper   1/8 teaspoon

Instructions:

1. Take a large frying pan, place it over medium heat, add oil, and let it heat until hot.
2. Then add spinach and tomatoes, cook until spinach wilts, pour in the eggs, stir until mixed and cook for 30 seconds.
3. Add cheese and then cook for 2 to 3 minutes until eggs have scrambled.
4. Season the eggs with salt and black pepper and then serve.

Quinoa with Berries

Prep Time:	5 minutes	Calories:	176
Cook Time:	60 minutes	Fat (g):	10
Total Time:	1 h and 5 min	Protein (g):	4.3
Servings:	4	Carbs:	19

Extremely healthy, filling, and delicious.

Ingredients:

- Quinoa, rinsed

    1 cup

- Olive oil, divided

    1 tablespoon

- Ginger, peeled, cut into coins

    One-piece, about 1-inch

- Salt

    ¾ teaspoon

- Lemon zest   1 teaspoon
- Mixed berries, fresh   1 cups
- Water   1 ½ cups

Instructions:

1. Take a large saucepan, place it over medium-high heat, add 1 tablespoon of oil and when hot, add quinoa and then cook for 2-3 minutes.
2. Pour in water, stir in salt, add ginger and lemon zest, stir until mixed, and then bring the mixture to a boil.
3. Switch to medium-low heat, simmer for 20 minutes, then remove the pan from heat and let it sit for 5 minutes, covering the pan with a lid.
4. Drain the remaining water and then fluff the grain with a fork, remove the ginger, spoon the grain on the large baking sheet, and spread evenly. Cool the grains for 30 minutes.
5. Serve with berries or chill it overnight and then serve the next morning.

Muesli

Prep Time:	10 minutes	Calories:	165
Cook Time:	12 minutes	Fat (g):	1.8
Total Time:	22 minutes	Protein (g):	4.5
Servings:	8	Carbs:	30.6

It is a perfect breakfast, which is filled with all the nutrients you need. It's toasty, nutty, and delicious to eat.

Ingredients:

- Rolled oats   3 ½ cups
- Wheat bran   ½ cup
- Salt   ½ teaspoon
                       ½ teaspoon

- Ground cinnamon
- Almonds ½ cup
- Hazelnuts ¼ cup
- Pumpkin seeds, shelled ¼ cup
- Dried apricots, chopped ¼ cup
- Raisins ¼ cup

Instructions:

1. Switch on the oven, then set it to 350 degrees F (177°C) and let it preheat.
2. Take a baking sheet, place wheat bran and oats in it, sprinkle with salt and cinnamon, toss until combined, and then spread the grains in an even layer.
3. Take a second baking sheet, place pumpkin seeds, hazelnuts, and almonds, toss until combined, and then spread the grains in an even layer.
4. Place both baking sheets into the oven and then bake for 10 to 12 minutes until fragrant.
5. When done, remove baking sheets from the oven and set them aside until cooled.
6. Then transfer all the ingredients in the baking sheets into a large bowl, add raisins and apricots and toss until combined.
7. You can serve it with Greek yogurt and honey.

Mediterranean Breakfast Quinoa

Prep Time:	5 minutes	Calories:	326.6
Cook Time:	20 minutes	Fat (g):	7.9
Total Time:	25 minutes	Protein (g):	11.5
Servings:	4	Carbs:	53.9

This dish is packed with healthy ingredients that you will need to start your day. It's nutty, toasty, and sweet to taste.

Ingredients:

- Almond flakes — ¼ cup
- Ground cinnamon — 1 teaspoon
- Quinoa — 1 cup
- Whole milk — 2 cups
- Salt — 1 teaspoon
- Vanilla extract, unsweetened — 1 teaspoon

- Honey   2 tablespoons
- Dates, pitted   2
- Apricot, dried   5

Instructions:

1. Take a medium saucepan, place it over medium heat, add quinoa, stir in cinnamon and cook for 3 to 4 minutes until thoroughly warm.
2. Then stir in salt, pour in the milk, and bring the mixture to a boil.
3. Reduce heat to the low level and then simmer for 15 minutes, covering the pan with the lid.
4. Add remaining ingredients except for half of the almonds, stir until mixed and cook for 2 minutes until hot.
5. Distribute quinoa among four bowls, top with remaining almonds, and then serve.

Spinach and Feta Egg Wrap

Prep Time:	5 minutes	Calories:	703.5
Cook Time:	5 minutes	Fat (g):	36.8
Total Time:	10 minutes	Protein (g):	36.6
Servings:	1	Carbs:	78

This breakfast wrap will satisfy your morning hunger. Creamy cheese and veggies will bring the taste and health to you.

Ingredients:

- Whole-wheat tortilla   1
- Coconut oil   1 ½ teaspoons
- Baby spinach   1 cup
- Eggs   2
- Feta cheese   1/3 cup
- Medium cucumber, diced   1

Instructions:

1. Take a large skillet pan, place it over medium heat and when hot, place the tortilla in it and then toast it.
2. Transfer tortilla to a plate, add oil to the skillet pan, switch heat to medium-high level and let it melt.
3. Add spinach and cook for 1 minute until spinach wilts, add eggs and then cook for 2 minutes until eggs have scrambled.
4. Sprinkle cheese over eggs, cook for 1 minute until cheese melts and then spoon eggs over the tortilla.
5. Top the eggs with diced cucumber, roll it like a wrap and then serve.

Fig and Ricotta Toast

Prep Time:	5 minutes	Calories:	252
Cook Time:	0 minutes	Fat (g):	9 g
Total Time:	5 minutes	Protein (g):	12 g
Servings:	2	Carbs (g):	32 g

Ingredients:

- Whole-grain bread, sliced — 2, about ½-inch thick
- Ricotta cheese — ½ cup
- Fig, sliced — 4
- Sea salt — 1/16 teaspoon

Instructions:

1. Warm the slices until toasted on both sides and place them on a plate.
2. Spread ricotta cheese, then top with figs and season with salt.
3. Serve.

Lunch

Mediterranean Cucumber Tomato Salad

Prep Time:	10 minutes	Calories:	105
Cook Time:	0 minutes	Fat (g):	7.5
Total Time:	10 minutes	Protein (g):	2.3
Servings:	4	Carbs:	9.8

This all-star salad is a great lunch option. It has parsley and lemony dressing to bring up the Mediterranean flavors.

Ingredients:

- Tomatoes, cut into wedges   3 cups
- Large cucumber, diced   1

- Chopped parsley leaves, fresh — ½ cup
- Salt — 1/3 teaspoon
- Ground black pepper — ½ teaspoon
- Ground Sumac — 1 teaspoon
- Olive oil — 2 tablespoons
- Lemon juice — 2 teaspoons

Instructions:

1. Take a large salad bowl, place cucumber, tomatoes, and parsley in it, stir in salt and let the salad rest for 5 minutes.
2. Then add remaining ingredients into the salad, toss until mixed, and then serve.

Greek Salad

Prep Time:	10 minutes	Calories:	103
Cook Time:	0 minutes	Fat (g):	9.5
Total Time:	10 minutes	Protein (g):	0.7
Servings:	6	Carbs:	4.7

This Mediterranean iconic dish is filled with crunchy, colorful veggies and soft cheese. It's one of Greek's finger-licking food.

Ingredients:

- 1 Red onion, medium, peeled, sliced in half-moons
- 4 Tomatoes, medium, cut into wedges
- 1

- Cucumber, peeled in a striped pattern, ½-inch thick sliced

  1

- Red bell pepper, medium, cored, sliced into rings

  2 oz (57 g)

- Lettuce leaves

  ¼ cup

- Black olives, pitted, halved

  1/8 teaspoon

- Salt

  4 tablespoons

- Olive oil

  2 tablespoons

- Red wine vinegar

  1

- Block of feta cheese, sliced in large pieces

  ½ tablespoon

- Dried oregano

Instructions:

1. Take a large salad dish, add onion, tomatoes, pepper, cucumber, lettuce leaves, and olives in it and then season with salt and oregano.
2. Pour oil and vinegar over the salad, toss until just mixed, top the salad with feta cheese.
3. Serve the salad with crusty bread.

White Bean Salad

Prep Time:	5 minutes	Calories:	205
Cook Time:	0 minutes	Fat (g):	6
Total Time:	5 minutes	Protein (g):	10
Servings:	4	Carbs:	31

This dish uses bright and colorful Mediterranean ingredients to fill your stomach.

Ingredients:

- White beans, cooked — 30 oz (850 g)
- Cherry tomatoes, chopped — 10 oz (283 g)
- Onions, chopped — 4
- Chopped parsley, fresh — 1 cup

- Leaves of mint, chopped — 20
- Lemon, zested, juiced — 1
- Salt — 2/3 teaspoon
- Ground black pepper — ½ teaspoon
- Za'atar — 1 teaspoon
- Sumac — ½ teaspoon
- Aleppo pepper — ½ teaspoon
- Olive oil — 2 tablespoons

Instructions:

1. Take a large salad bowl, place beans in it, and then add tomatoes, parsley, onions, and mint in it.
2. Season with salt and black pepper, add lemon zest, Aleppo pepper, sumac, and za'atar, and then drizzle with oil and lemon juice.
3. Toss the salad until just mixed, let it rest for 30 minutes, and then serve.

Mediterranean Couscous Salad

Prep Time:	5 minutes	Calories:	153
Cook Time:	25 minutes	Fat (g):	6.9
Total Time:	30 minutes	Protein (g):	4.7
Servings:	6	Carbs:	23

Made with hearty chickpeas and crunchy veggies, this couscous salad will elevate your lunch experience. It's also filled with herbs and has a light and zippy lemon dressing.

Ingredients:

For the Vinaigrette:

- Large lemon, juiced — 1
- Olive oil — 1/3 cup
- Dill weed — 1 teaspoon

- Minced garlic — 1 tablespoon
- Salt and pepper — 2/3 teaspoon
- Ground black pepper — ½ teaspoon

For the Salad:

- Pearl couscous — 2 cups
- Olive oil — 2 tablespoons
- Water — 3 cups
- Grape tomatoes, halved — 2 cups
- Cucumber, chopped — ½
- Yellow bell pepper, chopped — ½
- Kalamata olives, pitted, chopped — ½ cup
- Basil leaves, chopped — 15

Instructions:

1. Prepare the vinaigrette and for this, take a small bowl, place all of its ingredients in it and then whisk until combined, set aside until required.
2. Prepare the salad and for this, take a medium pot, add oil and when hot, add couscous and then cook for 2 to 3 minutes until golden brown.
3. Pour in the water, cook the couscous according to the package, and then drain it into the colander.
4. Take a large salad bowl, place remaining ingredients for the salad in it except for basil, stir until combined, and then stir in basil and couscous until mixed.
5. Drizzle the prepared vinaigrette over the salad, stir until just mixed.
6. Serve straight away.

Baked Parmesan Zucchini

Prep Time:	10 minutes	Calories:	67
Cook Time:	23 minutes	Fat (g):	3.3
Total Time:	33 minutes	Protein (g):	5.4
Servings:	5	Carbs:	4.8

Toasty and golden, these tender baked zucchinis are best served hot with a beautiful and healthy dipping sauce. The herbs and cheese bring out the flavors in this vegetable.

Ingredients:

- Zucchini, large, trimmed, cut into sticks length-wise — 4
- Olive oil — As needed

<u>For Parmesan-Thyme Topping:</u>

- Parmesan cheese, grated — ½ cup
- Thyme leaves, fresh — 2 teaspoons
- Oregano, dried — 1 teaspoon
- Sweet paprika — ½ teaspoon
- Ground black pepper — ½ teaspoon
- Salt — 1/8 teaspoon

Instructions:

1. Switch on the oven, then set it to 350 degrees F (177°C) and let it preheat.
2. Meanwhile, take a small bowl, place cheese in it, add all other ingredients for topping and then stir until well combined.
3. Take a large baking sheet, place a wire rack on it, brush it with oil, and then arrange zucchini pieces on it, skin-side-down.
4. Brush zucchini with oil, sprinkle with parmesan mixture and then bake for 17 to 23 minutes until golden and tender-crisp.
5. Serve.

Fish Sticks

Prep Time:	10 minutes	Calories:	119
Cook Time:	15 minutes	Fat (g):	3.8
Total Time:	25 minutes	Protein (g):	13.6
Servings:	14	Carbs:	8

This is an easy-to-make fish dish. These tender fish sticks are crispy and cheesy and flavorful from seasonings.

Ingredients:

- Fish salmon fillet, skinless 1 ½ lbs (680 g)
- Salt 1 ½ teaspoons
- Ground black pepper 1 teaspoon

- Oregano, dried — 1 teaspoon
- Sweet paprika — 1 teaspoon
- Whole wheat flour — ½ cup
- Egg, beaten — 1
- Bread crumbs — ½ cup
- Parmesan cheese, grated — ½ cup
- Olive oil — As needed
- Lemon, zested — 1
- Lemon, juiced — ½
- Parsley, chopped — 2 tablespoons

Instructions:

1. Switch on the oven, then set it to 450 degrees F (232°C) and let it preheat.
2. Meanwhile, season salmon fillets with salt on both sides and then cut it into 3-inch long pieces.
3. Take a small bowl, place paprika in it, stir in black pepper and oregano and then stir until combined. Season the pieces on both sides with this mixture.
4. Take a shallow dish, place flour in it, then take a separate shallow dish and whisk the egg in it.
5. Take a separate dish, place bread crumbs in it and then stir in lemon zest and parmesan cheese.
6. Dredge a fish piece into the flour until well coated on both, dip into beaten egg, dredge into parmesan-bread crumbs mixture, and place it on a greased baking sheet.
7. Repeat with the remaining fish pieces and then bake for 12 to 15 minutes until golden brown and fork-tender.
8. When done, drizzle lemon juice over fish pieces, sprinkle with parsley and then serve.

Falafel

Prep Time:	1 h 15 m + soaking time	Calories:	296
Cook Time:	15 minutes	Fat (g):	7
Total Time:	1 h 30 m + soaking time	Protein (g):	16
Servings:	6	Carbs:	52

This is a recipe of an authentic falafel, made with vegan ingredients and a mixture of high-quality spices. It's delicious, hearty, and healthy and makes a great lunch.

Ingredients:

- Dried chickpeas   2 cups

- Baking soda   ½ teaspoon

                                     1 cup

- Parsley leaves, fresh   3/4 cup
- Cilantro leaves, fresh   ½ cup
- Dill leaves, fresh   1
- White onion, small, peeled, quartered
- Cloves of garlic, peeled   8
- Salt   1 teaspoon
- Ground black pepper   1 tablespoon
- Cumin, ground   1 tablespoon
- Ground coriander   1 tablespoon
- Cayenne pepper   1 teaspoon
- Baking powder   1 teaspoon
- Sesame seeds, toasted   2 tablespoons
- Olive oil   As needed for frying

Instructions:

1. One day before cooking falafel, place chickpea in a large bowl, pour in enough water to cover peas by 2-inches, stir in baking soda and then let the chickpeas soak overnight.
2. Then drain the chickpeas, pat dry, and transfer them into a food processor.
3. Add onion, salt, garlic, parsley leaves, dill leaves, cilantro leaves, black pepper, cumin, coriander, cayenne pepper, then pulse for 40 seconds at a time until well combined, tip the mixture in a bowl, cover with its lid and let it refrigerate for a minimum of 1 hour.
4. When ready to cook, add sesame seeds and baking powder into the falafel mixture, stir until mixed, and then shape the mixture into ½-inch thick patties, about 24.

5. Take a deep skillet pan, place it over medium-high heat, pour in oil until 3-inches filled and when hot, add falafel patties in it, and then fry for 5 minutes or more until done.
6. When cooked, place patties on a plate lined with paper towels to soak excess oil and repeat with the remaining patties.
7. Serve falafel with salad.

Roasted Tomato and Basil Soup

Prep Time:	10 minutes	Calories:	148
Cook Time:	60 minutes	Fat (g):	6.6
Total Time:	1 h 10 m	Protein (g):	4
Servings:	6	Carbs:	22.7

This vegan soup is rich and delicious.

Ingredients:

- Roma tomatoes, halved 3 lbs (1 kg 361 g)
- Carrots, peeled, cut into small chunks 3
- Olive oil 4 tablespoons

1 teaspoon

- Salt
- Ground black pepper
- White onions, medium, peeled, chopped
- Minced garlic
- Crushed tomatoes
- Basil leaves
- Thyme leaves
- Oregano, dried
- Sweet paprika
- Cumin, ground
- Water

½ teaspoon

2

3 tablespoons

1 cup

2 oz (57 g)

2 teaspoons

1 teaspoon

½ teaspoon

½ teaspoon

2 ½ cups

Instructions:

1. Switch on the oven, then set it to 450 degrees F (232°C) and let it preheat.
2. Meanwhile, take a large bowl, place carrot pieces and Roma tomatoes in it, drizzle with 2 tablespoons oil, season with ½ teaspoon salt and ¼ teaspoon black pepper, and then toss until combined.
3. Take a large baking sheet, spread the vegetables (carrot pieces and Roma tomatoes) in a single layer, and then roast them for 30 minutes.
4. When done, let the vegetables cool for 10 minutes, transfer them into a food processor, pour in 4 tablespoons of water, and pulse until blended.
5. Take a large pot, place it over medium-high heat, add remaining oil and when hot, add onion and cook for 3 minutes until tender.
6. Add garlic, cook for 1 minute until golden, then pour in tomato mixture, stir in crushed tomatoes, salt, thyme, black pepper, basil, cumin, paprika, and oregano. Pour in the remaining water and bring it to a boil.
7. Then switch heat to the low level and simmer the soup for 20 minutes, covering the pan half with its lid.

8. When done, remove thyme from the soup, transfer the soup into bowls, drizzle with oil, and then serve with bread.

Mediterranean Tuna Salad

Prep Time:	10 minutes	Calories:	225
Cook Time:	32 minutes	Fat (g):	9
Total Time:	42 minutes	Protein (g):	32
Servings:	2	Carbs:	3

Ingredients:

For the Dijon Mustard Dressing:

- Dijon mustard — 2 ½ teaspoons
- Lime, zested — 1
- Limes, juiced — 1 ½
- Olive oil — 2 tablespoons

- Sumac — ½ teaspoon
- Salt — 1/8 teaspoon
- Ground black pepper — 1/8 teaspoon
- Crushed red pepper flakes — ½ teaspoon

For the Tuna Salad:

- Tuna, canned — 7 oz (198 g)
- Whole radishes, small, stems removed, chopped — 4
- Green onions, chopped — 3
- Olives, pitted — ½ cup
- Arugula — ½ cup
- Basil leaves, chopped — 15
- Cherry tomatoes, cut into wedges — 12
- Egg, boiled, cut into wedges — 2

Instructions:

1. Prepare the vinaigrette and for this, take a small bowl, place all of the Dijon Mustard Dressing ingredients in it, and then whisk until well blended, set aside until required.
2. Prepare the salad and for this, take a large salad bowl, place tuna in it, add all other ingredients except for the egg and then stir until mixed.
3. Pour the prepared vinaigrette over the salad, toss until evenly coated, cover the bowl with its lid, and then let it refrigerate for 30 minutes.
4. Top salad with egg wedges and then serve.

Italian Baked Chicken

Prep Time:	10 minutes	Calories:	270
Cook Time:	30 minutes	Fat (g):	9
Total Time:	40 minutes	Protein (g):	36
Servings:	6	Carbs:	11

Ingredients:

- Chicken breast, boneless, skinless — 2 lbs (907 g)
- Salt — 2 teaspoons
- Ground black pepper — 2 teaspoons
- Oregano, dried — 2 teaspoons
- Sweet paprika — 1 teaspoon

- Minced garlic — 2 tablespoons
- Olive oil — 3 tablespoons
- Lemon, juiced — ½
- Cherry tomatoes, halved — 6
- Chopped parsley, fresh — 2 tablespoons
- Garlic cloves — 6

Instructions:

1. Switch on the oven, then set it to 425 degrees F (218°C) and let it preheat.
2. Season chicken with salt and black pepper, and then place it in a large bowl.
3. Add minced garlic, paprika and oregano, drizzle with oil and lemon juice and toss until well coated.
4. Take a large baking dish, grease it with oil, spread garlic cloves in its bottom, top with chicken, and then scatter tomatoes on top.
5. Cover the baking dish with foil, bake the chicken for 10 minutes, then uncover it and continue baking for 10 minutes until tender and thoroughly cooked.
6. When done, cover the dish with foil, let the chicken rest for 10 minutes, then garnish with parsley and serve.

Stuffed Champignon Mushrooms

Prep Time:	10 minutes	Calories:	51
Cook Time:	20 minutes	Fat (g):	3
Total Time:	30 minutes	Protein (g):	2
Servings:	12	Carbs:	3

A stuff mushroom recipe filled with classic Mediterranean ingredients, tomatoes, spinach, olives, and cheese.

Ingredients:

- Olive oil — 3 tablespoons
- Minced garlic — ½ tablespoon
- Ground black pepper — ½ teaspoon
- Salt — ¼ teaspoon
- Champignon mushrooms, stems removed — 12

- Spinach, chopped — 1 cup
- Cherry tomatoes, chopped — ½ cup
- Feta cheese, crumbled — 1/3 cup
- Kalamata olives, pitted, sliced — 2 tablespoons
- Chopped oregano — 1 tablespoon
- Cheddar cheese, grated — ¼ cup

Instructions:

1. Switch on the oven, then set it to 400 degrees F (204°C) and let it preheat.
2. Meanwhile, take a small bowl, place salt in it, add garlic, black pepper, and 2 tablespoons oil in it and then stir until combined.
3. Brush the garlic mixture over mushrooms until coated, arrange them on a large baking sheet and then bake for 10 minutes until softened.
4. While mushroom bakes, take a medium bowl, place spinach, olives, and tomatoes in it, add oregano, feta cheese, and remaining oil and toss until combined.
5. When mushrooms have baked, stuff them with the spinach mixture, top with the cheddar cheese and then continue baking for 10 minutes.
6. Serve straight away.

Prosciutto and Arugula Pizza

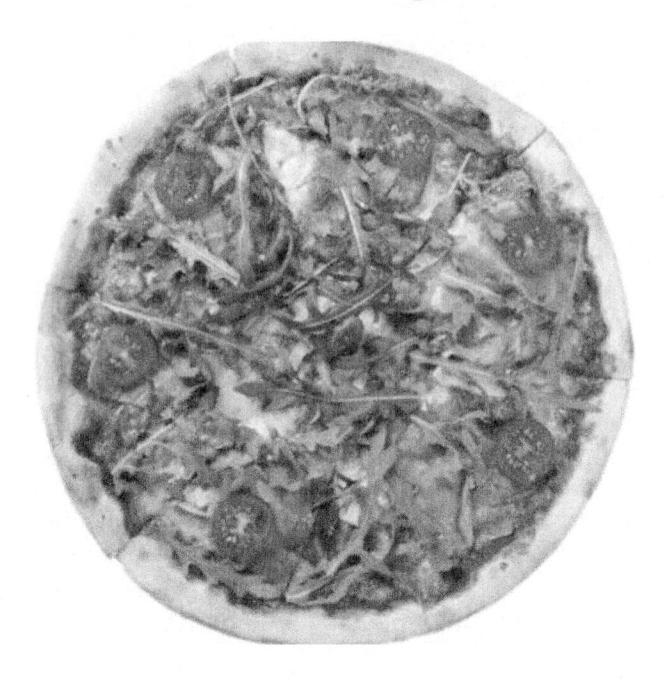

Prep Time:	5 minutes	Calories:	290
Cook Time:	20 minutes	Fat (g):	13.3
Total Time:	25 minutes	Protein (g):	12
Servings:	6	Carbs:	35.3

This is a simple pizza for the whole family.

Ingredients:

- Pizza dough, whole-wheat — 1 lb (453 g)
- Olive oil — 2 tablespoons
- Minced garlic — ½ teaspoon
- Mozzarella cheese, shredded — 1 cup
- Prosciutto slices, 1-inch sliced (you can use chicken instead) — 1 oz (28 g)
- Arugula — ½ cup
- Cherry tomatoes, halved — 1/2 cup
- Ground black pepper — ¼ teaspoon

Instructions:

1. Switch on the oven, then set it to 450 degrees F (232°C) and let it preheat.
2. Place the dough on a dusted working space; roll it into a 12-inch round shape.
3. Take a small bowl, place garlic in it, add oil and then stir until mixed.
4. Brush the baking sheet with oil, place the crust on it, and then spread garlic oil mixture on it, top with prosciutto, cherry tomatoes, and cheese.
5. Bake for 18-20 minutes until cheese melts and the bottom of the crust turn light brown.
6. When done, top the pizza with arugula, sprinkle with black pepper, drizzle with oil, and then cut it into slices.
7. Serve straight away.

Chicken and Spinach Pasta

Prep Time:	10 minutes	Calories:	334
Cook Time:	20 minutes	Fat (g):	12.3
Total Time:	30 minutes	Protein (g):	28.7
Servings:	4	Carbs:	25

Ingredients:

- Penne pasta, whole-wheat — 8 oz (227 g)
- Olive oil — 2 tablespoons
- Chicken breast, boneless, skinless — 1 pound (453 g)
- Salt — ½ teaspoon
- Ground black pepper — ¼ teaspoon
- Minced garlic — 2 tablespoons
- Dry white wine — ½ cup
- Lemon, juiced, zested — 1
- Spinach, chopped, fresh — 1 cup

- Alfredo sauce, divided   8 tablespoons

Instructions:

1. Cook pasta according to the package instructions.
2. Take a large skillet pan, place it over medium-high heat, add oil and when hot, add chicken, season it with salt and black pepper and cook for 5 to 7 minutes until thoroughly cooked.
3. Then add garlic, cook for 1 minute until fragrant, stir in wine, lemon zest, and juice and bring the mixture to a simmer.
4. Remove pan from heat, add pasta and spinach into the pan, stir until mixed and cover the pan with its lid; let it rest for 5 to 10 minutes until spinach leaves wilts.
5. Stir in Alfredo sauce until well mixed.
6. Divide pasta and chicken evenly among four plates and then serve.

Mediterranean Quinoa Salad

Prep Time:	20 minutes	Calories:	278.4
Cook Time:	20 minutes	Fat (g):	14
Total Time:	40 minutes	Protein (g):	18.4
Servings:	8	Carbs:	20.1

This is a healthy, light Mediterranean salad that can be made without chicken for vegans. It's filled with hearty quinoa, veggies, herbs, and lemon flavor.

Ingredients:

- Water — 2 cups
- Chicken broth cubes — 2
- Clove of garlic, peeled — 1
- Quinoa, dry — 1 cup
- Chicken breast, large, chopped — 2
- Green onion, diced — 1

- Green bell pepper, diced — 1
- Arugula — ½ cup
- Cherry tomatoes, chopped — ½ cup
- Parsley leaves, chopped — ¼ cup
- Salt — to taste
- Black pepper — to taste
- Lemon juice — ¼ cup
- Balsamic vinegar — 1 tablespoon
- Olive oil — ¼ cup + 2 tablespoons

Instructions:

1. Take a large saucepan, place it over medium-high heat, pour in water, add chicken broth cubes and garlic and bring the mixture to boil.
2. Stir in quinoa, switch heat to medium-low level, cover the pan with its lid and then simmer for 15 to 20 minutes until quinoa turned tender and have absorbed all the liquid.
3. Meanwhile, take a large skillet pan, place it over medium-high heat, add 2 tablespoons of oil and when hot, add chicken, season it with salt and black pepper and cook for 5 to 7 minutes until thoroughly cooked. Set aside until required.
4. When quinoa is done, remove garlic clove, fluff the quinoa with a fork and then transfer into a large bowl.
5. Add chicken into the quinoa, add remaining ingredients, and then stir until well mixed.
6. Serve straight away.

Penne with Shrimp

Prep Time:	5 minutes	Calories:	257.3
Cook Time:	7 minutes	Fat (g):	5.5
Total Time:	12 minutes	Protein (g):	16.5
Servings:	4	Carbs:	36

It is an Italian dish that is light and delicious. It is made with pasta and shrimp along with some veggies and cheese.

Ingredients:

- Penne pasta, whole-wheat — 8 oz (227 g)
- Olive oil — 1 tablespoon
- Minced garlic — 1 teaspoon
- Dry white wine — 1 tablespoon
- Cherry tomatoes, cut into wedges — 7 oz (198 g)
- Shrimp, peeled, deveined, fresh — 7 oz (198 g)

- Parmesan cheese, grated   ¼ cup
- Parsley, chopped   ¼ cup

Instructions:

1. Cook pasta according to the package instructions.
2. Take a large skillet pan, place it over medium heat, add oil and when hot, add garlic, shrimp, pour in the wine, and cook for 5-7 minutes.
3. Then add pasta, tomatoes, toss until mixed, then sprinkle cheese and parsley on top.
4. Serve straight away.

Dinner

Greek Red Lentil Soup

Prep Time:	10 minutes	Calories:	347
Cook Time:	30 minutes	Fat (g):	7
Total Time:	40 minutes	Protein (g):	19
Servings:	4	Carbs:	57

This is a Greek-style red lentil soup that is thick and rich. It is made of a tomato base, red lentils, and fresh herbs and spices.

Ingredients:

- Olive oil

3 tablespoons

- White onion, large, chopped

1

1 ½ tablespoons

- Minced garlic

  2
- Carrots, chopped

  3 teaspoons
- Oregano, dried

  1 ½ teaspoons
- Cumin

  1 teaspoon
- Rosemary

  ½ teaspoon
- Red pepper flakes

  2
- Bay leaves, dry

  1 cup
- Crushed tomatoes

  7 cups
- Vegetable broth

  2 cups
- Red lentils, rinsed and drained

  1 teaspoon
- Salt

  1
- Lemon, zested

  2
- Lemons, juiced

Instructions:

1. Take a medium saucepan, place it over medium heat, add oil and when hot, add onion, garlic, and carrots, and then cook for 4 minutes.
2. Add bay leaves, salt, and all the spices, stir until mixed, cook for 1 minute until fragrant, then add lentils and tomatoes, and pour in the broth.
3. Stir until mixed, simmer the mixture for 20 minutes or more until lentils have thoroughly cooked and then remove the pan from heat.
4. Let the soup cool for 5 minutes, then puree it by using an immersion blender until smooth and reheat the soup over medium heat until thoroughly warmed.
5. Add lemon juice, and zest, stir until mixed, and then ladle soup into bowls.
6. Drizzle some more oil into the soup and then serve.

Salmon Soup

Prep Time:	5 minutes	Calories:	340
Cook Time:	25 minutes	Fat (g):	11
Total Time:	30 minutes	Protein (g):	33
Servings:	4	Carbs:	31

This is an easy and light salmon soup made with potatoes and carrots.

Ingredients:

- Olive oil — 2 tablespoons
- Minced garlic — 2 tablespoons
- Dill, fresh, chopped — 1 teaspoon
- Chicken broth — 5 cups
- 8 oz (227 g)

- Potatoes, peeled, chopped into cubes

  4 oz (113 g)

- Millet

  1

- Carrot, peeled, chopped

  1 teaspoon

- Oregano, dry

  ¾ teaspoon

- Ground coriander

  ½ teaspoon

- Cumin, ground

  ¾ teaspoon

- Salt

  ½ teaspoon

- Ground black pepper

  1 lb (453 g)

- Salmon fillet, skinless, cut into small pieces

  1

- Lemon, juiced, zested

Instructions:

1. Take a large pot, place it over medium-high heat, add oil, and when hot, add garlic and dill, cook for 30 seconds until fragrant, add carrots, millet, and potatoes. Pour in the broth, season the soup with salt, black pepper, and all the spices and then bring the mixture to a boil.
2. Then switch heat to medium-low level and simmer the soup for 15 minutes or more until vegetables have turned tender.
3. Then season salmon pieces with salt, add them into the pot, switch heat to lower level, and cook the soup for 10 minutes until thoroughly cooked and fork-tender.
4. Add lemon juice and zest and then ladle soup into bowls.
5. Serve soup with a piece of crusty bread.

Greek Black Eyed Peas

Prep Time:	5 minutes	Calories:	188
Cook Time:	45 minutes	Fat (g):	3
Total Time:	50 minutes	Protein (g):	9
Servings:	6	Carbs:	33

This is a Greek-style stew, packed with flavors and can feed an entire family. Fresh herbs and a splash of lime bring the flavors together.

Ingredients:

- Olive oil — 2 tablespoons
- White onion, large, peeled, chopped — 1
- Minced garlic — 2 teaspoons
- 1

- Green bell pepper, cored, chopped

  3
- Carrots, peeled and chopped

  2 cups
- Water

  1
- Bay leaf, dry

  1 ½ teaspoon
- Cumin, ground

  1 teaspoon
- Oregano, dry

  1/2 teaspoon
- Paprika

  1 teaspoon
- Salt

  ½ teaspoon
- Ground black pepper

  ½ teaspoon
- Red pepper flakes

  30 ounces (850 g)
- Black-eyed peas, cooked

  1
- Lime, juiced

  1
- Chili pepper, chopped

Instructions:

1. Take a large pot, place it over medium heat, add oil, and when hot, add onion and garlic and cook for 5 minutes until tender.
2. Add carrots and bell peppers, stir until mixed, and then cook for 5 minutes.
3. Season with salt, black pepper, and all the spices, add bay leaf, pour in water, and bring the mixture to a boil.
4. Add peas, chili pepper, and boil for 5 minutes, then switch heat to the low-level and then simmer the soup for 30 minutes.
5. Stir in lime juice, remove the pot from heat and then divide peas evenly among bowls.
6. Serve with salad.

Baked Cod with Garlic and Lemon

Prep Time:	10 minutes	Calories:	318
Cook Time:	16 minutes	Fat (g):	18
Total Time:	26 minutes	Protein (g):	23
Servings:	4	Carbs:	16

This simple and quick recipe can easily become a regular in your dinner. Beautiful cod is seasoned with olive oil, garlic, and lemon juice to enhance the flavor.

Ingredients:

- Cod fillet pieces, about six pieces — 1 ½ lbs (680 g)
- Olive oil — 2 tablespoons
- Minced garlic — 2 ½ teaspoons

For Lemon Juice Mixture:

- Butter, unsalted, melted   2 tablespoons
- Lemon juice   5 tablespoons
- Olive oil   5 tablespoons

Instructions:

1. Switch on the oven, then set it to 400 degrees F (204°C) and let it preheat.
2. Meanwhile, take a shallow dish, add butter, oil, and lemon juice in it, whisk until combined, and then set aside until required.
3. Working on one fish piece at a time, dip it into lemon mixture. Repeat with the remaining pieces.
4. Take a large skillet pan, place it over medium-high heat, add oil and when hot, place fish pieces in it and then cook for 2 to 3 minutes per side until golden brown, don't cook.
5. When done, arrange fish pieces on a baking sheet.
6. Add minced garlic into the dish containing the remaining lemon mixture, stir until mixed, and then drizzle over fish pieces.
7. Bake fish pieces for 10 minutes until fork tender.
8. Serve and enjoy!

Greek Chicken Souvlaki

Prep Time:	2 h 10 m	Calories:	504
Cook Time:	10 minutes	Fat (g):	23
Total Time:	2 h 20 m	Protein (g):	66
Servings:	4	Carbs:	5.5

Present this juicy chicken dish at your table with beautiful dipping sauce.

Ingredients:

- Chicken breast, boneless, skinless   2 ½ lbs (1 kg 134 g)

For the Marinade:
- Cloves of garlic, peeled   10
- Dried oregano   2 tablespoons
- Dried rosemary   1 teaspoon
- Paprika   1 teaspoon
- Salt   1 teaspoon

- Ground black pepper — 1 teaspoon
- Olive oil — ¼ cup
- Dry white wine — ¼ cup
- Lemon, juiced — 1
- Bay leaves — 2

For Serving:
- Pita Bread — 4
- Tzatziki Sauce — 6 tablespoons
- Sliced tomato — 1
- White onion, peeled, sliced — 1
- Kalamata olives, pitted, sliced — ½ cup

Instructions:

1. Prepare the marinade and for this, place all of its ingredients in a food processor except for bay leaves and then pulse until well combined.
2. Cut chicken into 1 ½ inches pieces, place them in a large bowl, top with blended marinade, toss until well coated, and then let it marinate for a minimum of 2 hours.
3. When 45 minutes are left, take 12 wooden skewers and soak them in warm water.
4. Meanwhile, prepare and arrange the ingredients for serving.
5. When ready to cook, set the grill and then let it preheat over medium-high heat.
6. Thread chicken pieces into wooden skewers, brush the grilling grate with oil, place chicken skewers on it and then cook for 3 to 4 minutes per side until nicely browned on all sides and cooked, brushing marinade frequently.
7. When done, place chicken skewers on a plate and let them rest for 3 minutes.
8. Meanwhile, warm the pita bread on the grill grate until thoroughly warmed.
9. Working on one pita bread a time, spread 1 ½ tablespoon Tzatziki sauce on it, add chicken from two skewers and then top with tomato, onion, and olives. Prepare remaining pitas in the same manner and then serve.

Grilled Swordfish

Prep Time:	23 minutes	Calories:	395
Cook Time:	8 minutes	Fat (g):	31
Total Time:	31 minutes	Protein (g):	28
Servings:	4	Carbs:	2

This is a Mediterranean-style swordfish recipe, which is light and delicious. It has the taste of olive oil, herbs, and spices.

Ingredients:

- Swordfish steaks — 4, each about 6 oz (170 g)
- Cloves of garlic, peeled — 12
- Olive oil — 1/3 cup
- 2 tablespoons

- Lemon juice

    1 teaspoon
- Coriander

    ¾ teaspoon
- Cumin

    1 teaspoon
- Paprika

    ¾ teaspoon
- Salt

    ½ teaspoon
- Ground black pepper

Instructions:

1. Place garlic cloves in a food processor, add salt, black pepper, all the spices, lemon juice, and olive oil and then pulse for 3 minutes until the thick paste comes together.
2. Place steaks in a dish, spread the blended marinade on both sides, and then let it rest for 15 minutes.
3. Meanwhile, set the grill and let it preheat at a high heat setting.
4. When ready to cook, brush the grill grate with oil, place marinated steaks on it, and then cook for 5 minutes.
5. Turn the steaks, continue cooking them for 3 minutes until cooked and fork-tender, and then transfer steaks to a plate.
6. Drizzle some more lemon juice over steaks and then serve with potato.

Mediterranean Stuffed Chicken Breasts

Prep Time:	10 minutes	Calories:	182
Cook Time:	27 minutes	Fat (g):	8
Total Time:	37 minutes	Protein (g):	25
Servings:	8	Carbs:	2

Ingredients:

- Feta cheese, crumbled — ½ cup
- Spinach, fresh — ½ cup
- Kalamata olives, pitted, quartered — ¼ cup
- Chopped basil — 1 tablespoon
- Chopped parsley — 1 tablespoon
- Minced garlic — 1 teaspoon
- Chicken breasts, skinless, boneless — 4, each about 8 oz (227g)
- Salt — ¼ teaspoon
- Ground black pepper — ½ teaspoon

- Olive oil — 1 tablespoon
- Lemon juice — 1 tablespoon

Instructions:

1. Switch on the oven, then set it to 400 degrees F (204°C) and let it preheat.
2. Take a medium bowl, place garlic, spinach, parsley, olives, basil, and feta cheese in it and then stir until mixed.
3. Make a pocket into each chicken breast by making a horizontal slit, stuff each chicken with ¼ cup of feta cheese mixture, secure with toothpicks, and then season chicken with salt and black pepper.
4. Take a large skillet pan, place it over medium-high heat, add oil and when hot, place stuffed chicken in it and then cook for 2 minutes until golden.
5. Turn each chicken, place it into the oven, and then bake for 25 minutes until the internal temperature of chicken reaches 165 degrees F (74°C).
6. When done, drizzle lemon juice over chicken, remove the toothpick and then serve.

Greek Cauliflower Rice Bowls with Chicken

Prep Time:	10 minutes	Calories:	395
Cook Time:	19 minutes	Fat (g):	19
Total Time:	29 minutes	Protein (g):	29
Servings:	4	Carbs:	9

This salad can be made with or without chicken if you are a vegetarian. Filled with crunchy veggies and chicken, this dish can be made very easily.

Ingredients:

- Olive oil, divided — 4 tablespoons
- Cauliflower rice — 4 cups
- Onion, chopped — 1
- Salt, divided — ¾ teaspoon
- Parsley, fresh, chopped — ½ cup
- Chicken breasts, boneless, skinless, chopped — 1 lb (453 g)

- Ground black pepper, divided — ½ teaspoon
- Lemon juice — 3 tablespoons
- Dried oregano — 1 teaspoon
- Tomatoes, cut into wedges — 1 cup
- Red bell pepper, chopped — 1/3 cup
- Yellow bell pepper, chopped — ¼ cup
- Red chili pepper, chopped — ¼ cup
- Celery, chopped — ¼ cup
- White or green zucchini, chopped — ¼ cup

Instructions:

1. Take a large skillet pan, place it over medium-high heat, add 2 tablespoons of oil and when hot, add onion and cauliflower rice, season with ¼ teaspoon of salt, and then cook for 5 minutes until softened.
2. Remove cauliflower rice from the pan and set aside.
3. Take a large skillet pan, place it over medium-high heat, add 2 tablespoons of oil, and when hot, add chicken. Season it with the remaining salt, black pepper, and oregano and cook for 5 to 7 minutes until thoroughly cooked.
4. Then add celery, zucchini, red and yellow bell peppers, mix well and cook for another 2 minutes.
5. When done, remove the pan from the heat, add chili and mix well. Let it sit for 5 minutes.
6. Divide cauliflower rice evenly among four bowls, serve with the chicken mix, tomatoes, and parsley. Sprinkle with the lemon juice.

Chicken Parmesan Pasta

Prep Time:	10 minutes	Calories:	438
Cook Time:	22 minutes	Fat (g):	13
Total Time:	32 minutes	Protein (g):	33
Servings:	4	Carbs:	45

This one-pan recipe minimizes the effort and makes pasta making easy.

Ingredients:

- Olive oil — 2 tablespoons
- Minced garlic — 1 tablespoon
- Chicken breast, skinless, boneless, cut into ½-inch pieces — 1 lb (453 g)
- Italian seasoning — 1 teaspoon
- Salt — ¼ teaspoon
- Chicken broth — 3 cups

- Penne, whole-wheat — 8 oz (227 g)
- Parmesan cheese, shredded — ¼ cup

Instructions:

1. Take a large skillet pan, place it over medium-high heat, add oil and when hot, stir in garlic, then add chicken pieces, salt, and Italian seasoning and then cook for 2 minutes until chicken is no longer pink.
2. Add broth, and penne pasta into the pan, and then bring the mixture to a boil.
3. Switch heat to medium level and then cook for 15 to 20 minutes.
4. When done, sprinkle parmesan and then serve.

Mediterranean Chicken and Chickpea Soup

Prep Time:	10 minutes	Calories:	449
Cook Time:	8 hours	Fat (g):	15
Total Time:	8 h 10 m	Protein (g):	33
Servings:	6	Carbs:	43

Ingredients:

- Chickpea, dried, soaked overnight — 1 ½ cups
- Water — 4 cups
- White onion, large, peeled, chopped — 1
- Fire-roasted tomatoes, diced — 15 oz (425 g)
- Tomato paste — 2 tablespoons
- Chopped garlic — 2 tablespoons
- Bay leaf — 1
- Cumin, ground — 4 teaspoons
- Paprika — 4 teaspoons
- Cayenne pepper — ¼ teaspoon
- Ground black pepper — ¼ teaspoon

- Chicken breasts, skinless, chopped   2 lbs (907 g)
- Salt   ½ teaspoon
- Cilantro, chopped   ¼ cup

Instructions:

1. Place chickpeas in a slow cooker, pour in water, add remaining ingredients except for chicken, and salt and then stir until mixed.
2. Add chicken, cover the slow cooker with its lid and then cook for 4 hours at high heat setting or 8 hours at low heat setting.
3. Remove bay leaves from the sauce in the slow cooker, add salt, stir until mixed, and then ladle soup into bowls.
4. Serve.

Chicken Piccata

Prep Time:	10 minutes	Calories:	382
Cook Time:	13 minutes	Fat (g):	19
Total Time:	23 minutes	Protein (g):	38
Servings:	4	Carbs:	11

This is an easy and quick chicken recipe that can easily become your favorite. Bring Italy to your dinner table using this meal.

Ingredients:

- Lemon 1
- Chicken breasts, boneless, skinless 1 ½ lbs (680 g)
- Salt 1 teaspoon

1 teaspoon

- Ground black pepper
- Whole-wheat flour 1/3 cup
- Butter, unsalted, divided 3 tablespoons
- Olive oil 2 tablespoons
- Chicken broth 1 cup
- Capers 2 tablespoons

Instructions:

1. Cut the lemon in half, squeeze juice from one half of the lemon, and then cut the other half of lemon into slices, set aside until required.
2. Slice the chicken breasts in half lengthwise, season evenly with salt and black pepper, and then dredge into flour.
3. Then take a large skillet pan, place it over medium-high heat, add oil and 2 tablespoons butter and when it melts, add chicken in a single layer and then cook for 3 minutes per side until golden brown.
4. Transfer chicken pieces to a plate, cover it with foil and then repeat with the remaining chicken pieces.
5. Then switch heat to medium level, stir in chicken broth, add capes, lemon juice, and lemon slices, stir and cook for 7 minutes.
6. Stir in remaining butter until it melts, taste the sauce to adjust seasoning, and then ladle it over chicken.
7. Serve straight away.

Greek Turkey Burgers

Prep Time:	40 minutes	Calories:	389
Cook Time:	10 minutes	Fat (g):	13
Total Time:	50 minutes	Protein (g):	40
Servings:	4	Carbs:	31

These turkey burgers will go great with your favorite burger fillings. This recipe uses veggies and herbs that bring Mediterranean flavors to the table.

Ingredients:

For the Patties:

- Ground turkey — 1 lb (453 g)
- Spinach leaves, fresh, chopped — ½ cup
- Sun-dried tomatoes, chopped — 1/3 cup

- Red onion, minced — ¼ cup
- Feta cheese, crumbled — ¼ cup
- Minced garlic — 1 teaspoon
- Egg, whisked — 1
- Olive oil — 1 tablespoon
- Dried oregano — 1 teaspoon
- Salt — ½ teaspoon
- Ground black pepper — ½ teaspoon

For Serving:

- Hamburger buns, whole-wheat — 4
- Lettuce leaves — 4
- Sliced red onion — 1
- Tzatziki Sauce — ¾ cup

Instructions:

1. Prepare the patties and for this, take a large bowl, place all the ingredients in it except for salt, oregano, oil, garlic, and egg and then stir until just mixed.
2. Crack the egg in a small bowl, add garlic, oil, salt, and oregano, whisk until blended, and pour the mixture over turkey mixture and then mix until well combined.
3. Shape the mixture into four patties, place them on a plate lined with parchment paper, and then refrigerate the patties for a minimum of 30 minutes.
4. Then take a grill pan, place it over medium heat, grease it with oil and when hot, place the patties on it and then cook for 5 minutes per side until golden brown and thoroughly cooked.

5. When done, layer each bun with a lettuce leaf, top with a patty and some onion slices, drizzle with the sauce and then serve.

Greek Chicken Soup with Lemon

Prep Time:	5 minutes	Calories:	261
Cook Time:	19 minutes	Fat (g):	8
Total Time:	24 minutes	Protein (g):	32
Servings:	6	Carbs:	16

Try this satisfying, rich, and filling Greek chicken soup that comes together within 30 minutes. Feel free to swap orzo with your favorite grains.

Ingredients:

- Olive oil — 1 tablespoon
- Carrots, peeled, cubed — ¾ cup
- Chopped white onion — ½ cup
- Minced garlic — 2 teaspoons
- Crushed red pepper — ¾ teaspoon
- Chicken broth — 6 cups

- Orzo, whole-wheat — ½ cup
- Eggs — 3
- Lemon juice — ¼ cup
- Shredded rotisserie chicken — 3 cups
- Salt — 1 ¼ teaspoons
- Ground black pepper — ½ teaspoon
- Chopped dill — 3 tablespoons

Instructions:

1. Place a large pot over medium-high heat, add oil and when hot, add onion and carrots and then cook for 4 minutes or until softened.
2. Stir in red pepper and garlic, cook for 1 minute until fragrant, and then pour in the broth.
3. Stir until mixed, switch heat to a high level, and then bring the soup to a boil.
4. Add orzo into the pot and then cook for 6-10 minutes until tender, uncovering the pot.
5. Meanwhile, crack the eggs in a medium bowl, add lemon juice and whisk until frothy.
6. When orzo has cooked, remove 1 cup of broth from the pot, gradually whisk it into the egg-lime mixture until eggs have tempered.
7. Pour the egg-lemon mixture into the pot, stir until combined, and then switch heat to medium-low level.
8. Add chicken into the soup, season with salt and black pepper, and continue cooking for 1 minute.
9. Ladle soup into bowls, sprinkle with dill and then serve.

Shrimp Spaghetti

Prep Time:	5 minutes	Calories:	446
Cook Time:	15 minutes	Fat (g):	13
Total Time:	20 minutes	Protein (g):	28
Servings:	4	Carbs:	59

In this recipe, shrimp are served with a comforting sauce loaded with leeks and peas, making it a quick and impressive dinner. Serve it with the red wine.

Ingredients:

- Spaghetti, whole-grain   8 oz (227 g)
- Shrimp, peeled, deveined   1 lb (453 g)
- Ground black pepper   ¼ teaspoon
- Salt   ¼ teaspoon
- Olive oil   1 ½ tablespoons
- Minced garlic   1 tablespoon

- Cherry tomatoes, chopped — 2 cups
- Lemon zest — 2 teaspoons
- Lemon juice — 2 tablespoons
- Parsley, chopped — 2 tablespoons

Instructions:

1. Cook the pasta and for this, take a large pot half full with water, bring it to a boil over medium-high heat, then add spaghetti and cook for 7 to 10 minutes until tender.
2. Drain the spaghetti, reserve ½ cup of the cooking liquid, and set aside until required.
3. While spaghetti cooks, pat dry shrimp and then season them with salt and black pepper.
4. Take a large skillet pan, place it over high heat, add ¾ tablespoon of oil and when hot, add seasoned shrimp and tomatoes in it and then cook for 3 minutes per side.
5. Transfer shrimp and tomatoes to a plate and then keep them warm.
6. Switch the heat to a medium-high level, add remaining oil into the pan and when hot, add garlic, shrimp, tomatoes, and pour in reserved cooking liquid along with lemon zest and juice, stir until mixed. Simmer for 3 minutes.
7. Divide spaghetti evenly among four plates, top with shrimp. Sprinkle parsley on top.
8. Serve.

Tuna Patties

Prep Time:	10 minutes	Calories:	286
Cook Time:	10 minutes	Fat (g):	13.7 g
Total Time:	20 minutes	Protein (g):	32.8 g
Servings:	6	Carbs (g):	11.2 g

Ingredients:

- Tuna, canned, drained — 4 ½ oz (128 g)
- Eggs — 3
- Breadcrumbs — ¾ cup
- Onion, diced — 1/8 cup

- Olive oil — 4 tablespoons
- Lemon juice — 1 teaspoon
- Celery, diced — ¼ cup
- Ground black pepper — ¼ teaspoon
- Dill, chopped — ¼ teaspoon

Instructions:

1. Take a large bowl, place eggs and lemon juice in it. Beat and set aside.
2. Take another large bowl, place all the remaining ingredients except for olive oil, and mix well.
3. Pour in the egg mixture. Mix well.
4. Then shape the tuna mixture into patties, each about ½-inch thick.
5. Place a skillet pan over medium-high heat, add oil and when hot, add tuna patties and cook for 5 minutes per side or until nicely browned.
6. Serve.

Desserts

Balsamic Berries with Honey Yogurt

Prep Time:	10 minutes	Calories:	290
Cook Time:	0 minutes	Fat (g):	18
Total Time:	10 minutes	Protein (g):	14.6
Servings:	2	Carbs:	16.4

Ingredients:

- Blackberries — ¼ cup
- Blueberries — ¼ cup
- Raspberries — ¼ cup
- Balsamic vinegar — 1 tablespoon
- Greek yogurt — 1 ½ cup
- Honey — 2 teaspoons

Instructions:

1. Take a large bowl, pour vinegar in it, add all the berries, toss until coated with vinegar, and then let the berries sit for 10 minutes.
2. Then take a small bowl, place honey in it, add yogurt and then whisk until combined.
3. Divide yogurt honey mixture evenly among two bowls, top with berries, and then serve.

Yogurt and Honey Olive Oil Cake

Prep Time:	10 minutes	Calories:	260
Cook Time:	55 minutes	Fat (g):	12
Total Time:	1h 5 m	Protein (g):	5
Servings:	8	Carbs:	32

It's sweetened with honey and has a beautiful crumb.

Ingredients:

- Greek yogurt — 1 cup
- Olive oil — 2/3 cup
- Honey — 2/3 cup
- Lemon zest — 1 teaspoon
- Eggs — 3
- Whole-wheat flour — 1 ½ cups
- Baking powder — ½ teaspoon

- Baking soda ½ teaspoon
- Salt ¼ teaspoon

Instructions:

1. Switch on the oven, then set it to 325 degrees F (163°C) and let it preheat.
2. Meanwhile, take a round cake pan, about 9-inch, line it with parchment paper, grease it with oil, and set aside until required.
3. Take a large bowl, place yogurt in it, add honey, lemon zest, and oil and then whisk until combined.
4. Whisk in eggs, one at a time, and then stir in flour, salt, baking soda, and powder until smooth batter comes together, don't overmix.
5. Spoon the batter into the prepared cake pan and then bake for 45 minutes until the top turns golden brown and insert a toothpick into the cake comes out clean.
6. When done, transfer the pan onto a wire rack, cool it for 10 minutes, then take out the cake and cool it completely.
7. Cut cake into slices and then serve.

Apple and Nuts with Whipped Yogurt

Prep Time:	5 minutes	Calories:	302
Cook Time:	16 minutes	Fat (g):	22
Total Time:	21 minutes	Protein (g):	6
Servings:	4	Carbs:	26

A nutty, fruity dessert, made with Mediterranean ingredients.

Ingredients:

- Greek yogurt   1 cup
- Heavy cream   ½ cup
- Honey   2 tablespoons
- Butter, unsalted   2 tablespoons
- Ground cinnamon   1/8 teaspoon
- Apples, cored, cut into wedges   2
- Mixed nuts, chopped   ¼ cup

Instructions:

1. Take a medium bowl, place yogurt and cream in it, add honey, and then use a hand mixer to beat vigorously until the mixture thickens.
2. Take a large skillet pan, place it over medium heat, add butter and when it melts, add apple pieces, and then cook for 6 to 8 minutes until apples begin to soften.
3. Then sprinkle the cinnamon, continue cooking for 3 minutes, then remove the pan from heat and let the apples sit for 5 minutes until slightly cooled.
4. Divide yogurt-cream mixture evenly among four bowls, top with apples, and sprinkle with nuts and then serve.

Whole Grain Muffins with Citrus and Olive Oil

Prep Time:	10 minutes	Calories:	101
Cook Time:	20 minutes	Fat (g):	2
Total Time:	30 minutes	Protein (g):	2.1
Servings:	12	Carbs:	18.6

These are lightly sweetened, fluffy, and delicious muffins that will go great with afternoon tea or after-dinner dessert.

Ingredients:

- Whole-wheat flour — 1 ½ cups
- Rolled oats — ¼ cup
- Baking powder — 2 ½ teaspoons
- — ½ teaspoon

- Sea salt — ½ teaspoon
- Cinnamon — 1
- Egg — 1/3 cup
- Olive oil — 1/3 cup
- Orange juice, fresh — 1/3 cup
- Almond milk — 1/3 cup
- Maple syrup — ½ teaspoon
- Vanilla extract, unsweetened — ½ tablespoon
- Orange zest — ¼ cup
- Chopped almonds

Instructions:

1. Switch on the oven, then set it to 375 degrees F (190°C) and let it preheat.
2. Meanwhile, take a medium bowl, place flour in it, add oats, salt, cinnamon, and baking powder and then stir until mixed.
3. Take a separate medium bowl, crack the egg in it, add maple syrup, orange zest, and vanilla, pour in milk, orange juice, and olive oil and whisk until combined.
4. Whisk milk mixture into the flour mixture until incorporated.
5. Take a 12-cup muffin pan, scoop the batter in it, and fill evenly about ¾ full and then top with almonds.
6. Bake the muffins for 16 to 20 minutes until the top turn golden brown and inserted toothpick into the muffins come out clean.
7. When done, remove muffins from the pans, let them rest on the wire rack until cooled and then serve.

Baked Pears with Maple and Vanilla

Prep Time:	10 minutes	Calories:	179
Cook Time:	25 minutes	Fat (g):	2
Total Time:	35 minutes	Protein (g):	0.8
Servings:	4	Carbs:	40

A super simple, four-ingredient recipe.

Ingredients:

- Pears — 4
- Maple syrup — ½ cup
- Ground cinnamon — ¼ teaspoon
- Vanilla extract, unsweetened — 1 teaspoon

Instructions:

1. Switch on the oven, then set it to 375 degrees F (190°C) and let it preheat.
2. Meanwhile, cut each pear in half, core its seeds, and then cut a small sliver on the underside.
3. Place the pear halves on a baking sheet, cut-side-up, and then sprinkle with cinnamon.
4. Take a small bowl, place maple syrup in it, add vanilla and whisk until combined.
5. Drizzle the maple syrup over pear halves, reserving 2 tablespoons, and then bake for 25 minutes until the pears turn tender, and its edges have turned light brown.
6. When done, drizzle remaining maple syrup mixture over pears and serve.

Chocolate Mousse with Greek Yogurt

Prep Time:	10 minutes + chilling time	Calories:	282
Cook Time:	5 minutes	Fat (g):	18.2
Total Time:	15 minutes + chilling time	Protein (g):	5
Servings:	4	Carbs:	25.4

It's hard to believe this chocolate mousse is healthy, but it is. Made with Greek yogurt and a hint of vanilla, it will taste divine.

Ingredients:

- Coconut milk — ¾ cup
- Dark Chocolate, grated — 3.5 oz (100 g)
- Greek yogurt — 2 cups
- Honey — 1 tablespoon
- Vanilla extract, unsweetened — ½ teaspoon

Instructions:

1. Take a medium saucepan, place it over medium heat, pour in milk, add chocolate, and cook for 3 to 4 minutes until chocolate has melted.
2. Then add vanilla and honey into the milk and remove the pan from heat.
3. Take a large bowl, place yogurt in it, add chocolate mixture, and then whisk until well mixed.
4. Divide the mixture evenly among four ramekins and then chill in the refrigerator for 2 hours.
5. Garnish mousse with some berries and then serve.

Strawberry Popsicles

Prep Time:	10 minutes + chilling time	Calories:	100
Cook Time:	0 minutes	Fat (g):	1
Total Time:	10 minutes + chilling time	Protein (g):	4
Servings:	8	Carbs:	20

These mouth-watering popsicles are easy to make and great to munch on. Healthy and sweet, it will fulfill your sugar cravings.

Ingredients:

- Strawberries, fresh, hulled   2 ½ cups
- Almond milk, unsweetened   ½ cup

Instructions:

1. Place berries into a food processor, add milk and then blend until smooth.
2. Pour the mixture evenly into eight Popsicle molds, place a Popsicle stick into each mold and then freeze for a minimum of 4 hours until frozen.
3. Serve straight away.

Mint Chocolate Chip Ice Cream

Prep Time:	5 minutes + freezing time	Calories:	185
Cook Time:	0 minutes	Fat (g):	4
Total Time:	5 minutes + freezing time	Protein (g):	2
Servings:	4	Carbs:	35

This mint chocolate chip ice cream is healthy, nourishing, and creamy. Plus, you don't need an ice cream maker to prepare it.

Ingredients:

- Frozen banana — 4
- Salt — 1/8 teaspoon
- Peppermint extract, unsweetened — ¼ teaspoon
- Coconut cream — 1 cup
- Chocolate chips, sugar-free — 4 tablespoons

Instructions:

1. Place all the ingredients for the ice cream in a blender and then pulse until smooth.
2. Spoon it into a freezer-proof container, cover with its lid and then freeze for a minimum of 4 hours until firm.
3. When ready to eat, let the ice cream rest for 30 minutes until slightly soft, scoop ice cream into bowls and then serve.

Chocolate and Avocado Pudding

Prep Time:	5 minutes	Calories:	401
Cook Time:	5 minutes	Fat (g):	26
Total Time:	10 minutes	Protein (g):	5
Servings:	4	Carbs:	45

If you want something quick to satisfy your sweet craving, then chocolate and avocado pudding is the best to try. Serve it with your favorite toppings.

Ingredients:

- Avocado, large, chilled

    2

- Cocoa powder

    1/3 cup

- Maple syrup

    1/3 cup

    2 teaspoons

- Vanilla extract, unsweetened   ½ cup
- Coconut milk, full-fat, unsweetened   2 tablespoons
- Hazelnuts, chopped   ¼ teaspoon
- Sea salt

Instructions:

1. Cut each avocado in half, remove its pit and then transfer the flesh into a blender or a food processor.
2. Add cocoa powder, maple syrup, vanilla, and coconut milk and then blend until smooth.
3. Divide pudding evenly among four bowls, top each bowl with ½ tablespoon of nuts, sprinkle with 1/16 teaspoon of salt, and then serve.

Matcha and Blueberry Crisp

Prep Time:	10 minutes	Calories:	136.4
Cook Time:	25 minutes	Fat (g):	5.2
Total Time:	35 minutes	Protein (g):	2.5
Servings:	8	Carbs:	24.3

If you are a fan of matcha (powdered green tea), then this recipe is a great way to enjoy it as a dessert. Bake it for a party or a big family dinner and impress your guests with it.

Ingredients:

- Blueberries, fresh   10 oz (283 g)
- Arrowroot powder   2 teaspoons
- Cornmeal   1 cup

- Almond meal — ½ cup
- Shredded coconut, unsweetened — 1/3 cup
- Ground cinnamon — ¼ teaspoon
- Vanilla extract, unsweetened — 1 teaspoon
- Coconut oil, melted — 1/3 cup
- Maple syrup — 1/3 cup
- Matcha powder — 1 teaspoon

Instructions:

1. Switch on the oven, then set it to 350 degrees F (177°C) and let it preheat.
2. Meanwhile, take a 9-inch pie dish in an oval shape, place blueberries in it, stir in arrowroot powder, and spread evenly.
3. Take a large bowl, place remaining ingredients in it, stir until well combined, and then spread the mixture evenly over berries.
4. Place the pie dish into the oven, bake for 25 minutes or more until the top begins to brown, switch off the oven and then let the crisp rest for 30 minutes in it.
5. Serve straight away.

Conclusion

People live very unhealthily, and the only way to change is to inspire these people to take their health seriously. Education is a must, but they also need to be taught by example and be shown that it is not difficult and is worth it. Following this diet will not tax a person's energy or emotion; they will not be limited to eat a few amounts of food. Instead, the diet encourages eating until appetite is filled and receiving good nutrition and energy from healthy sources that do not have side effects.

Making a lifestyle change is a difficult choice but necessary if you want to reap the benefits of almost five decades of research.

I wish luck to anyone who has chosen to walk down the self-improvement path and have decided to follow the diet.

Printed in Dunstable, United Kingdom